THANK GOD –
FOR MY
BREAKDOWN?

Walter Riess

NORTHWESTERN PUBLISHING HOUSE
Milwaukee, Wisconsin

Library of Congress Card Number 79-91964
Northwestern Publishing House
3624 W. North Ave., Milwaukee, Wis. 53208
©1980 by Northwestern Publishing House. All rights reserved
Published 1980
Printed in the United States of America
ISBN 0-8100-0114-4

THANK GOD — FOR MY BREAKDOWN?

Contents

Preface

By the Doctor in Charge

There is a wisdom all her own in these words: *God moves in a mysterious way his wonders to perform.*

Surely no one could be more aware of that than we who call ourselves physicians. We don't have the power to cure — only to channel the forces of healing to the right place at the right time in the right way.

But while we work to find the channel, we have the infinite privilege of seeing mysterious forces beyond our comprehension bringing about the cure.

If ever I needed a renewal of my faith, it started several years ago when I met and assumed the care of the author of this quite incredible book. His problem had begun so insidiously, the result of overwork, tension, deadline pressures — all finally bursting into full and agonizing bloom. No matter where Reverend Walter Riess went for help, the answer was the same: chronic, viciously depressive illness, with an extremely bleak prognosis.

No future, to speak of, seemed in the offing.

More than once during the next two years it would have been much easier to call it quits, to admit defeat. But somewhere deep inside this man there seemed to be a bottomless well of faith the likes of which we had never seen before. And he just refused to give up, convinced there must be a reason in his Lord's own will for the otherwise unexplainable torment. Surely his Lord Christ must have a need for him later, *so he must survive.*

He did survive. With his tremendous God-given faith Pastor Riess fought his way back to the bright horizon of reality. And after it was done, the meaning of it all came to light.

Walter Riess had been put through the blackest of nights so that he could, from his own experience, help others keep hoping. For the One who gave us life, and redeemed life — physical and emotional life — stands so absolutely near, so absolutely to be trusted, and believed and loved into timelessness.

This book could have been written only by one who had plumbed the depths of such dreaded diagnosis. I pray that his encouragement and contagious spirit will renew hope in others who have felt the lash of a great crippler — a crippler known to one extent or another by one out of four Americans.

To the author himself I offer my gratitude for a great work well done. I use the word *great* for a single adequate reason: Pastor Walter Riess has managed to catch in these pages both the cold hurt and the warming healing of what he has gone through. No writer and no pastor, and no man who has made a life of being both, could face a sterner challenge.

The fact that he could face it, and did, says all I need to say about why I pray the same blessing for others.

It is possible to have your faith and your hope revived by a kindred spirit that will not say quit.

Reverend Walter Riess has quite a witness still ahead of him.

Dr. Harry E. Rinefort
Grosse Pointe, Michigan **9**

10

This is for my doctor.

Yea, though I walk through the valley of the shadow of death, I will fear no evil: for thou art with me; thy rod and thy staff they comfort me.

Psalm 23:4

The View from Space Craft One

It was the night before the Sabbath. Dust from the
road running southward from Jerusalem filtered up
into the reddish maze reeking of dried blood, some of
it thickening the lips that now begged for water from
people who held water — in goblets just out of the
reach of craning necks. Six beams of cheap wood,
flung together to get this thing over with before the
Sabbath itself came out of the humid sunset, shaped
three disjointed emblems of pain.

The mugs of water held out of reach, the odor of
sweat that would come no more and blood dried to the
lips, the necks pounding with the headaches that told
the coming of dying, the sticks of jagged wood, were
merely scenes of coming attractions astride a filthy
hill.

The shallow rise outside the pride of all Jewry had
done everything well to earn its name. Golgotha. The
Place of the Skull.

Somewhere under the blanket of offal that forever
crowns The Hill may still be buried some fragments of
the petrified hulks of wood that once held fast the feet

and the arms of the Man who dared to call himself the Son of God, the *Christus Rex.*

The tightly woven threads of pain that led into the dying did not shroud with calfskin tenderness the face of the Condemned, but bound to the wood the horror that ate at the roots of the tongue and the brain and the eyes. Until the whole agonized torment of it melted together to become part of the splinters. And part also of the mute shame itself that threaded down the slope and through the curious who had the stomach left to jeer, through the soldiers who had nothing left to guard but their own sullenly unpredictable urges to cry, or laugh, or run, the lonely walkers on the highway wrestling with themselves to convince each other and the clusters of onlookers —and maybe even the shapeless naked figures hanging on the wood —that they, innocent strollers, couldn't care less. And maybe they didn't. The thing going on to the side of them happened so often.

The only continually foreign sight was the puppet-dance and the strangely unbecoming cursing that dying by crucifixion carried with it. Cursing from the *wood* of all places. For when the nerve-ends of the body strung or strapped or nailed to a fourth-class plank gave way, what was left was wretched hate. Such hate could persist in that numbing last state for an hour, or even a day, or maybe two days. The accursed whose suffering would never be understood or shared could relish the guilt and fear cloaking the faces below like wash hanging out to dry under cloud and wind.

Only now something was wrong. You felt it in the nervousness of the crowd. Things were not going according to the Roman plan for the scenario for the executed.

One of the figures, the One with the paper still flapping above him — one of the bent hairpins of human flesh curling along the wood — would not help make the executioners feel things were worthwhile by adding his voice to the foul language flowing now from the other two crosses.

His last chance to prove himself a man, and what good comes of it? His guaranteed Bill of Rights to spit back at the mass of organized cruelty below his legs, the pitiful crucified-in-their-own-lust longing to be relieved by being cursed at, and nothing happens.

Worse than nothing. The man was saying love. *He was saying love.*

He was hanging them all on a cross that no one would ever be able to erase from the cursed Book that some fools were bound to write.

Who could resist hating this kind of talk, rolling in waves of contagious idiocy down the slope from the cross? This Man was not even man enough to damn and so free the puzzled, confused, suffering, despising corpses now searching each other for support —*any* support — to help them bear this fresh burden of love. The crucifiers could do no more to hurt him. They could torture him no more. They had to take the love talk and eat it whole.

But at that precise moment a mercy comes to their rescue.

The Talker of love is dead.

Nobody talks much about the next days. The days in the grave.

Every now and then someone claims the finding of it. On any Easter morning you can hear "In Joseph's Lovely Garden" rising above one of the squares of sod on this ball of earth where the grave lies hidden to this day. But nobody knows for certain where.

A weary astronaut arcs across the grubby few miles of Israel floating away backward below the view from his cramped quarter. Maybe for an instant his faith narrows to one fact that is indisputable. For that moment the intruder into the unbroken sky looks down at a clump of grass, or weed, or dust that is now the spindle on which turns all history.

Jesus Christ lay here. Or here. Or here. In death he lay.

Now the lonely clod of soil is empty. Hollow as most of the days we let go, hollow as most of the boredom we accept as "entertainment" in television, or Hollywood, or New York productions, or no productions at all.

The earth is stricken with relic-seekers now, or souvenir-hawkers, or religious faddists. But for a while, for just the days between Sabbath Eve and Easter morning, the pivotal Person of all the experience of mankind rested still and straight and without pain under one dry patch of clay, crumbly to the fingers, a mere flick of the lens to the cameras of Space Craft One.

The man and the God Jesus Christ then walked out into the world to say: "You are new. For I have tasted death, and the grave, and new life. And I am back with you to stay.

"Hold on to me and you will know what it is to be born all over again. I will not leave you the same. I know what it is like to lie in that earth. I know what it is to ache so much you long to lie down in it — and yet quiver with fear at the thought of it.

"Yet here I am, so alive that I offer my life to you. I go with you not just there, not just to the dust of the earth. I go with you all the way.

"I go with you to eternity — to an eternity of life.

"So you do not have even a tick of the watch to fear."

Slowly the full realization dawns on us. We no longer cringe in the face of life. Or in the face of death. Not in the view of the grave.

We do not go alone. We are never alone.

That's what the Savior can mean.

Space Craft One is gone by now.

But the faith of the ones who hear the words of this strange Voice from the patch of grass that death leaves in its wake — that faith will still hurl real Life into the cockpits of the space crafts that swirl over Israel.

That faith says now, as never before: Watch.

Watch, and pray and see with your own eyes that your Redeemer lives.

18

Keepers of the Message

Doctors like Harry Rinefort have heard Christ's talk of love.

How little I realized what a difference it would make.

Funny how you can still hold things together for a day or two when the best men in the field tell you it's all over.

I walked out of the banquet room of the Statler-Hilton in St. Louis, and it was raining softly all the way to the car. I remember not caring that my suit was wetting down to my skin. I remember that I could not think in words.

That was after the roast beef dinner, when my church's Board of Parish Education said goodbye in many fine words.

I walked to the car in the rain.

The phone was ringing at midnight when I got home, but there was no message. I sat down in the family room and listened to the rain.

A little while later I had things together in the car. Dr. Harry Rinefort's home was six hundred miles away, no more.

I didn't think a thing in words on the highway. It was still raining.

When I saw the man in his office I brought him a long white envelope from Dr. Troy Yost. The envelope said that I had Addison's disease. This is a failure of the adrenal glands and characterized by weakness, low blood pressure and discoloration of the skin.

Dr. Rinefort didn't look at the white paper. He started talking.

"Honest, Walt, every time I get out on that boat of mine at Elk Lake, I know *for a fact* that God's just *got* to be in control of everything.

"And you know, I have this feeling about you." He pauses to put all his weight (and it's considerable) on a particular vertebrae that somehow got out of kilter. "You know what it is, Walt?"

For another half-minute neither of us says a thing. Then: "It's a conviction I have — and maybe you being a preacher know what kind of a conviction I mean.

"Walt, I have this feeling that even if you fell into a bucket of manure, you'd come up smelling like a rose."

I can't laugh. I'm in no mood to share the conviction. Not this first visit.

"All right, preacher. Here it is. I've got this feeling in me that you're going to be doing things again. You wait and see. You're going to start feeling better, Walt.

"*Better*, friend, maybe better than you've been able to remember feeling for months."

An ultra-violet light switches on behind me, controlled by some invisible finger owned by someone in the office who's decided the conversation is enough for today. The light warms down on the place where the almost daily migraines are cutting a path up to my brain every afternoon about two.

"Do you follow me, Walt?"

I follow him. I follow his warmth and his unashamed care about his patients and his talk about his feelings. I still can't think in words, but I stay there trying to hear. Maybe I can memorize some of this, because there seems to be some healing warmth in it.

It's a strange thing to hear Harry Rinefort talk, if only because of that warmth. You feel it coming through the talk in spite of, not because of what he says. The words just come pouring out of him like the waters that froth into the shoreline below our home, down where the bay keeps the borders of our life.

Once or twice a year Harry Rinefort comes by Grand Traverse Bay, on his way to Rapid City where he has a lake home. He stays away from the city for a week, maybe two weeks.

When he comes here his face is drawn, and his skin more pale that it seems it ought to be. He looks as tired as the pastor he let come into his office that day after the roast beef banquet.

I remember thinking that day that there just might be some healing hidden away in stock and easy words. Anniversaries. Retirements. So, put things on tapes for typing out at the end of nine hours of other office words. Read a letter at night, if your office nerves don't leave you too plain tired out.

But the readers of the letters are at a loss. They do not know what Harry Rinefort knows: that a good doctor's words of healing come with a pain all its own. His pain draws from the marrow because the doctor is going through all that his people are going through.

I have the blessing to go to a doctor who knows Jesus Christ at better than secondhand. So Dr. Rinefort hears even the sighs between the words that gave our Lord Christ more pain than can be put in words. Here is one doctor who catches the real person around and beneath and underneath any amount of words. Other doctors may give you reams of notes to prove the full range of their clinic chrome machines. Harry will give you the full range of yourself — after he's sifted through all the words that clouded the windshield of your car on the way in.

Some of Us Shouldn't Be Here — Yet We Are

Before Rinefort, there was no real doctor as far as I was concerned.

In the first clutch of panic, that most intense of all pain called *breakdown*, the terror of feeling utterly lost makes pure cowards out of any and all of us.

I lost no time in getting to the nearest M. D. And yes, it is true: all doctors possess the same medication. But it is also true: all doctors have different words to say when the medication is being used by people. For now, it is enough for me to record that the Family Doctor Around The Corner does not really equal the deity we all have been conditioned to believe he is.

But there is another rather sad fact to put down, black on white, for anyone suddenly stricken by a disabling nervous attack. There are at least two dozen varying schools of "therapy" in existence in the United States today. My local doctor may easily have swallowed whole one or the other of these, possibly to my everlasting regret.

A single county in California, for example, boasts — boasts? — over thirty competing approaches to nervous ailments. That's one approach for every two thousand residents of this area near San Francisco. (The county also happens to be the most wealthy county, per capita, in the entire nation.) Each of the programs of therapy is well patronized. Each supports a medical staff free to claim that it is peculiarly well equipped to alleviate the distresses of the suffering.

Just for the record also, I spent an hour the other day combing through a long white envelope scrawled "Medical Record" which I kept behind the sliding doors of my writing table — just to make sure that I remain dutifully reminded of what my Lord Christ has delivered me from. In the course of treatment, by the record of this envelope, I have been recommended into experiencing seven distinct and variant systems of therapy. (An additional two were suggested to me by one doctor, both of them so obviously outlandish that even my desperate mood would not allow me to buy them.)

Yet I kept looking. I had to. Until a few years ago, even as late as two years ago, I did not know the physician who wrote the preface for this book. I did know several eminent doctors in the St. Louis, Milwaukee and Detroit areas, including the chief physician of one of the largest auto companies in the world.

But I was looking for someone who could be concerned enough about the well-being of a patient to spend an occasional evening making notes on that one patient's progress. I was looking for what turned out to be a humble, altogether human, and unassuming physician in a set of run-down, back offices on the second floor of a building on East Warren Avenue in Detroit.

First Touch of White on Gray

Before I met Harry Rinefort there was the moment when the gray flickered across another doctor's face. His eyes took on the distant look that most doctors have to cultivate — if only to protect themselves from pain they can neither accept in themselves nor heal in another.

I felt at the time as if it were a sin to be asking for help. I was convinced nothing more could be done. There was nothing to look forward to on that late afternoon, nothing but the raw traffic scraping along angrily out in the streets, and then the night alone in the city bedroom, curtains blowing to kill the sultry heat. What more could be said?

I walked down the stairway into the streets of gathering dark. My car stood where I had left it a million years ago, resting at the curb as if it knew all along what the answer, or lack of answer, would be. The dashboard stared back at me mimicking the doctor, eyes shaded and lights fading, hope gone.

The key was in the ignition, and I didn't move to turn it. The end of all hope in a doctor leaves all too much time to stare at the curious train of images spotting the windshield, spinning the past into globes of red and blue, now and then a glaring garish white. Some of the cars coming at me, careening by — some of them surely driven by those who had once listened to me fumbling with the Word of God on Sunday mornings. There would be no more fumbling now.

"Though he slay me, yet will I trust him," I mumbled from the book of Job. The lights seemed to flow all around, glistening over and above the gray mask of the doctor. With a brilliance strange to me they blotted out the incredible grief of the illness leading to the mask. "Though he slay me, yet will I trust him," I said again, and for the first time noticed that one particular image colored the windshield.

It was the image of a fire glowing in a cottage hearth. Above it spanned a loft with a single mattress on a bare wooden floor: a place where a boy of seven might see, if he tried very hard, the pages of a book, and might dream that life itself could be as eternal and meaningful as the lake outside, spiderlike in all its hundred outlets, throwing open its breast to the skies.

There in front of the office still under the impact of the grayness of that doctor's face — an impact that shocked everything inside me into focus — I found myself concentrating on only one saving picture: the rafters of a cottage roof, faintly red with the reflecting of the fire still in the hearth, and now still red and calling for an attention all its own amid the mindless scramble on the windshield. Atop those rafters a boy read his book, sensing beyond the pages the realness of all eternity in everyone and everything around him, an absolute imperishability of life breathed in and sustained by a thousand almost-silent waves lapping on the shore below him.

Now, at 4:39 in the morning, the rain and the thunder rumbling out on the Old Mission Peninsula quietly remind me of that cabin and the feverish sense of consecration that filled me there.

My father had put together enough savings to give us a week at a cottage here when I was seven. The rates at the end of August went down just enough to let a minister bring his family to south of the Mackinac ferry. But already the cloudy moods swelling the waters of Northwest Lower Peninsula were stiffening with cold. It was enough to start my mother fearing for the cabin stove.

I got out the book in the loft of the cottage, found a flashlight that worked, and read a line that would never let me rest content with illness of any kind.

The writer Aldous Huxley said that faith gave saints who lived on it a kind of transparent, reedy health. So those who banked their whole lives with a fire-love for Jesus Christ could reach a white heat in their companionship with Him.

This state of intense flame could burn to a cinder any stuff of sickness that might attack human flesh and blood and mind and spirit.

I read this under the roof of the cabin. There were no windows in the loft. The rain slashed there as if it were trying to get at the wood bracing up under the shingles. The book under the flashlight's yellow circle looked small in the noise of the storm. But the thing Aldous Huxley was saying was a thing I was to see played out years after that storm cleared. And I still see it played out, now, when Harry Rinefort takes a while to come out of his clinic rooms and into his private office, or maybe talks with me in the back yard of his Elk Lake home. I see under the furrows dredged in his face an absolutely fantastic will to keep in himself a relish for life itself.

I stand up poorly alongside such a man with his flare for life in the face of all the surrender to defeat that he sees in his own office waiting room. But I think that Mr. Aldous Huxley goes a long way in explaining at least what makes a man like Rinefort possible — and what makes a man like myself hopeful.

There's not a pauper's chance that I will ever know the grace of full healing. The migrainous arthritis left from a breakdown that still nauseates will not do a mystical-magic disappearance for a miracle-worker in a tent or a thousand of them in a temple. The Apostle Paul himself spoke the word of healing to others. But he never lied himself into believing that he would pray his own Savior into reversing the final answer, not even to salve a "thorn in the flesh" that made every step an agony for the chief messenger of the church.

My grace is enough for you, Jesus Christ said.

There would be no other word on the epilepsy, or the glaucoma, or whatever it was that forced Doctor Saint Luke to walk the painful roads with the Apostle. *My strength is complete in weakness.* There must have been times when Saint Paul wept with puzzlement and frustration at the verdict from his Lord Jesus. No doubt there were crowds that went unpreached to, and meetings that went unattended, and towns that were crossed off on the map, simply because Paul could not take any more pain that day. Or maybe the whole week. Or maybe — in terribly extreme emergencies — the whole unforgiving month.

Doctor Harry Rinefort knows what that is like, too.

He won't tell you, but he has cancer. Skin cancer.

In all the time I've known him, the doctor himself never told me that. I had to find it out from a friend of a friend, who heard it quite by chance. And with that a new chapter in the private, inner biography of my friend and doctor was added to my mental library.

The Humble Scenes of Healing

To find my doctor I had to climb the longest flight of stairs this side of Grosse Pointe, Michigan. A dingy hallway squared off to the right at the top landing and led darkly into a waiting room of more than average size, I suppose, but less than average equipment.

Financial blurbs from somewhat later than the depression era, brochures sent free and in lavish quantities from all sorts of medical firms, yesterday's *Free Press* topping the clutter, gave a fairly accurate idea of how Doctor Harry Rinefort despised the idea of any patient waiting in a lounge for any doctor.

He wasn't for it, to put it gently. In fact he seldom let people sit there more than ten minutes, if that. And if that, his secretary might as well as not apologize to you for the unreasonable delay.

And this didn't mean that you were scuttled in and out of the treatment room after a three-minute pre-boiled prescription made things ready for the next in line. The humble doctor stayed in the middle-income range because he scheduled you for about thirty to forty minutes. After such a going-over, which might have added a bit to the files of Mayo Clinic, the father might think to remind you that you owed anywhere from ten to twenty dollars. You got a receipt, so that even your ten or twenty dollars came back *via* insurance. And you walked down the long, long stairs to where your car was almost always overparked by one of those hour-limit dial things that bought and sold you for a nickel.

By noon you were home. This alone was pure miracle, if you know anything at all about Detroit doctors. You were also forty to sixty dollars richer, and infinitely wiser. In one *shorter* session at a local member of the Healing Arts, I got handed a bill for seventy-four dollars, some of them ostensibly for X-rays taken on the M. D.'s private office machine — a pretty file-full of negatives that were quite obviously his pride and pleasure. Unfortunately that brought me to a hospital for a colonoscopy that drove me into spasms of screaming because the doctor forgot to administer a single tablet for agonies that eventually cost me a hundred twenty-nine dollars and ninety cents more.

Harry Rinefort never charged me more than ten, and along with that told me he still missed the days when professional courtesy kept any pastor from getting a medical bill. Even then, once I stayed over an hour and twenty minutes because the patient next in line failed to show. But then, Dr. Rinefort never did save up enough money to buy one of those table-turning X-ray machines, and the stiff-backed wooden chairs in his office never felt comfortable for my abnormally long legs. I chose to remain standing while I waited for my receipt.

Which I would gladly have gone without. Dr. Harry Rinefort was the only person alive who could make me walk down those bleak stairs wanting to live when

I got to the bottom of them. That was more than I could say for the professional down the street. I never failed to wonder at the hidden gift of the doctor on East Warren Avenue who somehow managed to help when the mass of X-rays, packed away in immaculate boxes, couldn't quite cut the mustard — much less make you feel like going down the longest steps in Detroit two-at-a-time.

I never told him, simply because anything I could have told him would have been sheer guess work. How do you say to someone who has been blessed with witnessing the Lord's own healing touch that the essence of it all may lie in the hands that work by order of a brain carrying within itself faith only as large as a grain of mustard seed. And somewhere in his own cancer-ridden, tired, yet strangely healing self this mustard-grain of faith will persist in showing up — often at the oddest moments. It'll show up in the radically changed bodies and minds of patients who have no idea in the world that they are being brushed by the feather-tips of angels' wings.

So I did not go into explanations, or into profuse thanks. I thought of it, and gave up the notion of trying to put into words what can't go into words.

Whether he likes it or not there isn't another word that describes this doctor better than "healer" — that concept which has gone steadily lower in repute ever since Biblical times. Today it jostles against all our medical, psychological and spiritual fashion of doubting our lives away amid a mass of "existential anxiety." (You can't possibly opt for anything else *but* "existential anxiety" once you admit that you know nothing for sure about how your life is guided, or whether it's guided in the least by anything other than Capricorn and Aquarius.) In other words, faith has become an all but forgotten word.

But a Christian doctor like Harry Rinefort is a healer indeed, because the Lord Jesus Christ made him so. Yet if you took a recorder to his office, you wouldn't catch a whisper of all this. You'd drive off with your precious tapes, load up your stereo and scratch your head that you could be so gullible.

Healers like Harry have nothing going for them. Harry himself has confessed being perplexed that half the members of nearby Bethany Lutheran Church have come to him. He hasn't the faintest idea why this should be. This is one of the finer points about the medical practice of my physician-friend.

The Treatment Itself:
This Stubborn Life Eternal

One of the many complications a physician faces in treating a clergyman is the ease with which the man of medicine can tumble onto the exceedingly pointed horns of a painful dilemma.

If the patient does not make a recovery, the naturally warm friendship between doctor and minister can only suffer a deep sadness. On the other hand, if the patient refuses to capitulate to his illness and does bound back into the arena of life, he has regained all the equipment he needs to keep a doctor talking into all hours of the night.

Against such an onslaught a doctor's only defense is his ability to outtalk the now-renewed clergy into submission. That's roughly comparable to keeping a member of the Senate quiet with a Public Works Bill for his state coming up for a vote.

Doctor Harry Rinefort will not admit to any special brilliance in handling my years in his care. Yet the truth is the opposite.

Let me illustrate.

On my very first visit to his office, I handed Doctor Rinefort a thick envelope containing diagnoses, treatments and prognoses made by the small and the great of medical professionals from Missouri to Wisconsin to Michigan. The papers included a battery of test results from two medical laboratories, one in East Detroit, and the other in Pontiac, Michigan.

Not a single one of the diagnoses was considered curable. Doctor Rinefort knew that better than I. But he treated the envelope as if it didn't exist.

As I recall, he threw it in his file and informed me —several weeks later — that he "hadn't got around to reading it carefully."

But by that time the doctor had decided on a course of his own, comprehended in the following truths:

1. No such hope as a medical "cure" existed for any of the documented items belonging to my medical file.

2. Therefore I could hope only for a *relative* improvement, at best, for most of the conditions extant.

3. Most surely the way ahead to even a relative improvement would be filled with continuing pain, ominous setbacks and the use of possibly hazardous medications. Already one doctor had taught me to self-administer cortisone in large daily injections, prescribed by him for months ahead.

4. Doctor Rinefort's own immediate and practical concern was therefore to raise the level of my threshhold of hope — at least to the point where he might contemplate seeing me regularly for consultation and treatment.

The final insight of Doctor Rinefort was, I think, crucial to the whole course of treatment. But there never was a moment during the entire relationship we had together when I did not realize how central this was:

5. Since most of the symptoms, physical and otherwise, indicated the presence of conditions beyond cure, the doctor would concentrate all possible attention on the *spiritual* resources of the patient.

We started to talk. On the basis of these principles, we took on the job of talking *life* together.

I discovered I had a doctor who could survive the mass of laboratory statistics that might have totally demolished another physician amid a welter of considerations.

To put it in a word, I discovered an immense and bottomless and crystal clear conviction in an ancient Christian truth. It happened to be a truth that had not ceased to dominate my thinking since my Confirmation, or before.

The truth is called *Life Eternal.*

But to me the saving impact of this faith, this conviction, came from sheer amazement that a man of the medical profession had arrived at the ability to see everything —both in himself and in the world around him — under the aspect of this force he knew intimately. From the Bible he knew eternal life personally, as an experience of tremendous force and vitality.

It was in our talking together that we both, doctor and patient, came to witness what actually propelled the lives and survival of both of us. At one point Doctor Rinefort and I found ourselves assenting together: Eternal life is the one blessing that Jesus Christ gives earliest in life — to all of his own.

"It's never interrupted," I said.

"Not even in the grave."

The life eternal that defeats all illness and all sadness succeeds in seeping through the walls of a tomb.

38 But it is a most wonderful thing to know this — while you're still this side of heaven. Such is the assurance our Lord Jesus gives, for he is "the Resurrection and the Life."

Enough for a Thank You After

Long before I learned the meaning of pain, I used to
walk through the side door of Bethany Church, down
the longest aisle in Christendom, then take a right
through the door marked with a sign of rich-veined
oak wood: PASTOR'S OFFICE.

Inside were arm chairs of plush black leather,
mimeo hidden discreetly next to my gown and stoles
in the study closet, desk of polished brass and wood
facing the entrance, kneeling pad directly to the right
and guiding through the door to the chancel: altar,
pulpit, lectern, organ, all blessed by the prayers of a
stream of Bethany saints through their years of living. For years people have walked down these tiles to
talk with The Pastor about a daughter beat half to
death in the first week of her marriage; a son killed
playing Russian Roulette; a family of drunken sons
lying in a row in front of their mother's deathbed.

I've seen the likes of that in Ozark shacks as well,
but somehow done with more dignity than amid the
screaming traffic and exhaust of downtown Detroit. I
saw more dignity for the dying even by the Saint Clair
River, where a picnicker thoroughly under the weath-

er plummeted to his death from a circus balloon. But I am from birth unable to shrug off the sight of a grotesque tumbling of limbs to a drunken death ten feet from me. All I could do afterward was walk back to my sacristy office and fondle helplessly a blank sheet of typing paper. And no words came.

I don't suppose that it mattered. The room near the altar seemed enough. There was time for prayer in such a place.

We may understand that our pain lies a thousand fathoms deeper than our closest friend can detect, or accept, much less comprehend. But only the surrounding glow of God's purpose for us, and his Presence through every cell inside us (*Please, Lord Christ, no migraine today!*) can keep us moving through any morass of swamp that may muck up our steps today.

I know. I know for a sureness safe enough to be put on paper that the Light of our Savior Christ's Presence leaves enough for a thank you to him — even after the most fearful threat of all has been ours to face.

That threat is the terror of death.

Doctor Harry Rinefort says, "I'm not a preacher."

And he is the one who opened up for me the floodgates of my Lord's own grace-in-the-face-of-death.

But Harry Rinefort claims he is no preacher.

Yet without him I could not have looked at the Bethany pulpit one more time. Or done one more page. Or dared to take on one more thought in the stream of thoughts that had come to a sickening, unexplainable, and (humanly speaking) beyond-repair blockage on that one night of *Breakdown*.

When it came time for me to stare straight into the eyes of death — much because of the cortisone needle and its two cc. per day — it was Harry Rinefort who took it on himself to stare with me. And, finally, to stare death down.

That's when the thanks started to well up naturally in me again. After years in deep-freeze. After two years of another doctor's prediction that *any* facet of faith would not change by a second the hopeless way things were with me.

And he let me know they were hopeless.

Another doctor had said how cortisone kills kidneys. This doctor, rigorously trained in the halls of Berlin, said how religious faith doesn't do much to fill the void when hope goes.

Harry Rinefort said how we might as well start giving thanks.

We were still, after all, *alive*. We were so much alive, in fact, that the cortisone needles looked a little silly —and the Berlin doctor's bleak advice looked even sillier. (Machiavelli* was his best answer to the mysteries of getting along as a human in our kind of world.)

The strange thing is that I don't to this day regret seeing a single doctor in the chain of doctors that led up to Harry Rinefort. *Anyone* who helped me move on to him is all right in my book. Besides, how else do you get an education so complete that you *feel* the pain of a colonoscopy as totally as you *feel* the pain of reading Nicolo Machiavelli *for hope* when it's hopeless?

I give thanks for all of them. And for all the patient advisors in my church's pensions and support offices

*Nicolo Machiavelli (1469-1527) — Italian statesman who advocated political principles of craftiness and duplicity.

who sent the checks that paid about 80% of the colonoscopy as well as the medical lecture on the hope supposedly lurking in old Nicolo.

Come to think of it, I've never yet met a doctor who isn't a preacher, too. All medicine is hooked to faith like a trailer to a hitch, whether we like it or not. My friend from Berlin had as much faith in Machiavelli and Goethe** as Harry Rinefort in Jesus Christ. The only difference is that the doctor from Germany never seemed to notice how much his wagon was being pulled along by his slightly rusty gods.

I never could say that Harry Rinefort didn't know who was pulling his wagon.

For that, "Praise the Lord!"

I'll always be willing to take a part in that kind of thanksgiving.

What Harry Rinefort showed me — with good medicine and with a masterpiece of Christian personality — is how to live thanksgiving even on a migraine-threatened morning.

That makes quite a sermon, coming from a doctor.

But believe me, if I can get changed by it — in spite of the way I feel even about the dentist's drill — anyone reading this book is a candidate for the *Saved by the Grace of Thanksgiving*.

Praise the Lord.

Amen.

**Johann Wolfgang von Goethe (1749-1832) — great German poet and dramatist.

The Quiet Miracle

Depression in an emergency waiting room is something you can smell like smoke.

I admit I've got a thing about hospital lobbies — especially when they're vacant. Then the only other person yawning is the desk receptionist who's been up all night waiting for the blue van to throw in the wired bundle of morning newspapers.

Maybe it's because I'm so scared inside that the Lord brings me there even when I don't expect to be going.

Like for a recent 9:00 a. m. meeting that I couldn't forget if I tried. It happened after a night of Chinese lanterns burning up my elbows and knees and lower and upper back, and then into the neck muscles (you know where they are) where the lanterns suddenly blazed into flares that made my head incoherently migraine until the hurt dowsed all the Chinese paper lights with a thousand-milligram dose of whatever it took to make me want to die.

Migraines usually do. They hurt so bad — so my messenger of mercy Harry Rinefort tells me — as to match anything any human being can put up with.

You stare with flat fish-eyes at the lobby wall across from you (they're all painted foggy green, aren't they?),and you keep praying, "Dear Lord Christ of God — You know what the cross was like. You know I'd do anything to shake this torment. Only please just show me what to do. How to talk with the doctor trying to help — how to say anything clear to him through the crevice in my skull. Anything."

Well, by now the doctor is standing in front of you and you're trying to get it all out and in sifting through it all the doctor is learning more than Albert Schweitzer in Africa. You hope.

Then he talks and you quit hoping. The doctor's own pain is starting to show. He got up late this morning for surgery, cancelled putting on his socks and his breakfast to make the operating room in time. He sits with you now among the deserted gray-green chairs and walls of the waiting room. The receptionist is making noises with her gum. The phone has given up bothering the soggy atmosphere.

"How," the doctor is saying, "did it come on this time?"

This time, you think, *it was a little different.* "This time it was my knees and elbows. The elbows the worst. That worried me. Like yellow-hot floating globes of pain. So thick the stuff spread to the backbone. Then up into the back of the shoulders again. Then lower. Then up into that same back part of the neck I wish the Good Lord had forgotten — if only because it's sent me gagging to the toilet at least four thousand times since high school."

"Those knees and elbows," he says. "What about that?" He looks at me like a dishevelled secretary, slumping there with his legs crossed and his notebook on the high knee and his ankles almost a humorous white under the neon and the dignified gown. And I tell him all I can gather from the quick-flickering episodes strung like faded color slides all the way back to a seven-year-old boy lying in the attic of a North Michigan cottage, or to a second-story dormitory room on a Milwaukee campus where the boy later heard the diagnosis from a sweet-faced deaconess: "I'm afraid you have a simple case of tennis elbow." and the boy could not even respond: "But I don't *play* tennis!"

The flitting images go on, relentlessly, but I can't pretend to collect or assimilate the kaleidoscope that twirls in my mind. Even my body — all of fourteen —shivers in gangly helplessness before the first on-slaughts of pain. A particular kind of pain. Not tennis elbow — but the kind that gets other boys to laughing at your uncontrollable elbows flailing around on the basketball court. Or the time after a softball game when it seemed impossible to face the agony of walk-ing, just *walking* for God's loving sake, from a camp dining room to the barracks. All of it was saying something. But all of it came from people who didn't really know to a boy who had no possible right to object — especially to object with a word eons beyond medical science, the boy, and the boys on the team.

The word was arthritis.

Back now in the lounge, there is no air of excite-ment, much less of expectation, to make me hope for anything more than the good deaconess was able to give. The truth is that I am tired of the whole utterly routine game: the cheap copy of the ancient Greek dance. The doctor steps this way; I step this way. The doctor steps the other way; I step the other way. Even the doctor (bless him for not saying so) must be weary enough by now of the charade.

And then he says something that will echo through my deepest dreams and my slightly shallower note-books until I take it with me to the halls of eternity.

"We do know — fairly recently, as a matter of fact — that there is a form of arthritis that somehow stimulates migraine attacks. Even latent arthritis," he goes on in sanctified composure, "in a certain form can go that route." He pauses and I wait. "And really, until that form of arthritis manifests itself sharply enough [I loved that word 'sharply'] the entire process is exceedingly difficult to diagnose.

"I have reason to believe," he monotones on, his notebook still poised above the incongruous ankles, "that this condition is at the root of your situation."

Amen.

I catch myself about to shake my head in disbelief. I've got to get something clear to myself. After a half-life of the kind of embarrassing misery I wouldn't allow for my dog (Dolly went to the vet for the last time when she snarled with rheumatism), please, are you now carving the handle for grabbing hold of this thing? Are you promising that I'll never again have to stare down into my upstairs toilet bowl and wait to retch when there's nothing that will retch, and when afterward all I can pray (if I am still able to pray at all that night) is, *Savior Christ, can't you somehow tell me what this is all about?*

Arthritis.

The prayers retched out over the toilet bowl upstairs were heard.

I know it now, a little while later, when the six hundred milligram calciums and the number threes to go with the Nalfon flow out of the healing warming friendship with the man Harry Rinefort in Detroit and *his* friend Robert Gardner by the Bay here, in Traverse, and all of it together — the warming, the friendship, the healing, the flow — in some way brings us together in the kind of thing that could too easily degenerate into "The Doctors."

I'm too tired for that. I've still got a thing about hospital lobbies. If I were to plan the plot for a healing session — or even a session (like mine) on the *way* to a handle on the un-healable — I could dig up a better place for it all. As it is, the receptionist is still enjoying her gum, immensely. The doctor drifts hazily over to the elevator where he stands staring at the bottom button. The papers are lying on the floor.

The lobby is still empty. But I am not afraid any more. I feel like I am walking out in the presence of Someone who is at my side.

When Faith Joins with Faith

Yet without my wife Ingrid, Doctor Harry could not have helped the way he did.

If I keep silent at this moment, I can hear beyond the soft breathing of my wife an even softer sound of comforting assurance: the ceaseless and half-distant and not quite muffled washing ashore of the swellings of Grand Traverse Bay.

I could open the drapes that Ingrid made for the sliding picture windows at the peak of the A-frame here on the second story of our home. Then I could see clear across to the shore lights dotting the sands, like diamonds lying haphazard and almost careless on the velvet texture of night. Then I could see the pier lanterns where Ingrid and I walked our first night here, each of us secretly praying that our Lord Christ might somehow find a way to give us to live here. We had looked at all the islands of Hawaii, and at Puget Sound and San Francisco, and at Tucson's Navajo country and Canada's Cedar Point country, and now we knew we were home.

We had come here for healing.

Ingrid married me with the knowledge that our time together might be less than a year. My physician then, a good man in heart and mind, could come to no other answer than Addison's disease. Ingrid's sister had died from it, and complications, a few months before our marriage.

Especially since the death of Ullie, I kept reading the now almost incredible Scripture that said outright, *He healeth all my diseases.* I could not believe that God did not mean that for me, even now. I could not find death for me in my Bible — not on any page of it. Instead, when I kept returning for help for whatever in that Addison's disease diagnosis was drowning me in depression, I kept confronting a single incomprehensible line.

The words are from the second verse of Psalm 127: He gives to his particular loved ones in their *sleep.*

There was something almost beyond human reason hidden in the portrait of the Savior in his being with those who need him the most. The words toll softly a promise so still and so absolute that you have only one choice. Either believe his reach for you, or close the Book on your Lord for good.

But then what for me, and what for Ingrid, if the presence of the Christ I had lived and breathed and preached and written all my life proved unable to fulfill such promises? How could I hope for enough years to take with me my slim German girl, with her simple and unconditional faith, into what would all too soon be a second widowhood? Do you foist on such a trusting spirit a travel-home to carry you the last hundred miles, and carry along the books that blot the ink on prescriptions for pain? Do you try to ignore the tender puzzlement searching you from eyes of a woman who believes that ministers stand as symbols of faith in a world of un-faith? And how do you pray for the forgiveness you need for the reality with which you have buttressed your soul against the going of the light?

These are the questions looming now, when I finally do slide open the window curtains, and see alongside the careless and unforgettably haunting shore lights the passing months of the last year. I can pray again now. But then, there were no words to exorcise the torment. I had, as a matter of quiet fact, started to prepare myself to slip away into the dark with as few misgivings as possible. But my preparations were laughs thrown back into my own face. My despair was so deep I could feel no sadness, only a frozen blue numbness.

The worst of it is that despair — by any measure the most painful and wretched cloud settling over Addison's or any other disease — makes a near-farce out of even an *effort* to pray a few words of faith. What Winston Churchill called "the black dog," and what another writer called the "eternal three a. m.," does not yield gracefully to the resurrection of religious certainties slaughtered by pain. It is no surprise to me that Henry Francis Lyte wrote the lines of "Abide With Me" between such attacks of depression that he was hospitalized to save him from suicide. Such a hymn of faith as this came from a mind more acquainted with the hell of grief than the glow of joy over sureness about the here and the hereafter — and even the past.

So it was not a simple thing to beg, on my knees now so stiff with doubting, for the way to follow with

Ingrid. For the courage to go that way with whatever my prayers might bring me to. And then for *Ingrid* to have the courage to undertake again a wedding that might — by every purely human standard — prove to be a wake. One physician persisted. He even had

52 *insisted*, in utter candor and kindness, that Ingrid and I could surely live and love together without opening ourselves to the sorrow that marriage would bring. Surely, he reasoned, any one of my fellow clergymen would understand that, under these circumstances.

I'm not so sure that the good doctor knew too much about Lutheran pastors — at least not pastors of a certain root and branch. Yet the questions made sense. They might even have proved workable, for some clergy who had not, as I, come to experience the fullness of what love for a woman can be. The suggestions might have shown themselves in good light to a brother who could restrict love to a mutual satisfying of physical desire: I want you. I take you. I can convince myself that this is enough for a Christian give-and-take between a Christian man and a Christian woman.

One doctor said it could be that way. He was wrong. I could not even think it could be that way.

And then, quite suddenly, all the vari-colored pieces of our marriage fit together. I awoke one morning to the crystal clearness that it was all true. *He gives to his beloved in sleep.* I awoke to the given truth that, Addison's or no, Ingrid and I had but one road of faith stretching before us. We both realized what no doctor could say outright.

He could not speak for God.

It wasn't long after that that another doctor said something different.

Breakdown:
It Can Happen to Anyone

What we call nervous breakdown is all tied up with loss of "self-concept," which is all tied up with the way your parents saw you when you were born (or maybe even before), and which is the way you see yourself at such a deep level of your being that you can't even detect how you're thinking is affecting your being, your working, and now — your illness.

I went to school at a seminary. In those days no self-respecting preacher's son did anything else. I got a dollar a week in the mail. That had to pay for mailing laundry kits, getting haircuts, buying uniform buckles, dating girls, and buying an occasional hamburger to supplement the pathetic school menu, contributed by local farmers from the stock they couldn't get rid of on the open market.

But I wasn't the poorest of the poor. There were students who wore hunger on their faces while they tried to hone their minds rigorously on Latin texts, Greek and German, and things to be mastered that stretched beyond the normal boundaries of adolescent education year after year of English and American literature, history, algebra, geometry, botany, zoology, forensics, and of course, psychology, counseling, sociology. And all of this plucked rather at random from a veritable fog of theology. We covered

all the theological ground from Martin Luther's *Small Catchism* to Martin Chemnitz' great *Examen*, most of the meaty stuff there still untranslated.

Do we have any notion of the wisdom of years hidden in the gray matter of our brain? Do we have the slightest idea of what pure gold lies unmined in that ninety per cent of our brain that we never use?

I'm a pastor. I deal with people searching vaguely for help, and talking just as vaguely to me when they get to hinting about their search. I am always surprised at the abilities and gifts people carry around inside themselves — without the smallest vision of what these treasures are worth. To me the most outrageous criminals in the world are the so-called business executives who keep their underlings' salaries at the lowest possible pitch, while at the same time making absolutely sure that *no* executive happens to get a compliment that might possibly raise his or her self-esteem a single notch.

America's business community, with all its organizational and productive genius, long ago bought a bill of goods that makes this situation possible. Zeal for the dollar devours us. We are raised on the myth that earning the dollar is worth just about anything we do to our body or mind, or both, to get it. And because we are raised on that myth, we crack up by the dozens rather than try to make the switch to see ourselves in the light of eternity.

Yet our life's work is almost sacred to any of us. That is as it should be. For our calling comes from no one else but God himself.

Our day's effort is more than just a paycheck — it is something we breathe in just as naturally as a fish takes water through its gills, and just as needfully. The approval of our partners, the smile of a wife or the nod of a husband, are as vital as food and water.

Inwardly we know it. And not all the raucous assertions of The New Freedom, or the weirdly spiraling divorce rate, or the craze to hand life over to the Daily Astrology Forecast, can free us from our Lord's own stated will that we "replenish the earth, and subdue it; and have dominion over the fish of the sea, and over the fowl of the air, and over every living thing that moveth upon the earth."

From the start, God put into us the High Call to be creative. That is, he wants us to use the gifts he has given us. And we *all* have gifts.

No one knew this better than the Reformers and the Puritans. No one knows it better than the Christian martyrs.

And last of all, as of one born out of due season, I knew it.

The heartache of not being able to write — not a single word — with confidence or hope or joy, came on me with the breakdown. Frustration lay on me like a chain anchor coated with calcified mud.

I slogged about in Bunyan's Pit of Despond, agonizingly aware that a man unable to do his work — whatever his worthwhile work might be — could under no circumstances call himself a healed man. Or even a man on the way to healing.

After the floodgates collapsed, I could look at the tools of my trade, ministerial or literary, with only an ominous nausea. At last I stacked my pens and notebooks in my closet, where they stayed for months that eased into each other like oil into oil. Only Ingrid, my indomitable little German bride, refused to accept my feeling that all of it would have to be tossed, all the writing things once so much a part of me.

The Lord had given me to do some graciously accepted writing and editing. Now I could taste the chemistry of writing, but this time clearly out of order from the trauma, coming up sour in my mouth. Some hidden grace kept insisting that Ingrid, who had never in her life written more than a letter, had the right side of the argument. But surely there would never be another morning when I would wake anxious to see the lines marching again across the paper, now so carefully and uselessly preserved in the oblivion of the closet.

Yet the truth remained and refused to budge that scarcely any day could be satisfying that did not have some written creation — *something* from the depths of me — done in it. For creating gave the day its very color, its depth of shading, its rainbow tinting of a canvas that lasts through eternity itself. Like a fresh gleaming insight into my morning Psalm, my lines of the hours that died otherwise in futility would pulse on patiently and yet so excitingly through the drabness of the dullest boredom I might face.

But first, whether I liked it or not, the stocks of once-hopeful bond paper had to come down from the strange companionship with the hats, the ties, the cufflinks, and be placed squarely on the writing table in front of the living room fireplace, and there something done with them. *Something,* as I said before. Something that might, with prayer, bring me back to that flowing of hot blood cherished by any writer who wants to write, and not just dream vaguely of writing tomorrow.

Something today.

At first the paper, now down from the closet in one bold move, refused the most potent ritual I could bring to it. The stuff sat there, on the table, but so terribly inert — daring me to put down a single word that might break through the ice jam left behind by a winter of discontent. Then, but with extremely uncomfortable resistance, the mass started to give way. So rigidly, so slowly, so frustratingly *daily* — but it did start to give way.

"All right," I said to myself, "there are still the things I can do." The fiddling with "organizing folders." The checking of the fillers in my editing pens. The sheer planting of myself in the living room sofa: two hundred-plus pounds of dead weight. Then. . . the writing. Even bad lines, awkward words, if you will. But writing.

Patience has never come easily to me, not even when the writing was good. The writing itself was like sitting in a boat, and holding a line into the Dead Sea, not knowing that the water had been empty of fish for a thousand years. Yet going on, staying with the ridiculously lonely display of unrewarded fishing. That was what it was like.

Writer, I thought. Whoever was first to call himself *writer?* No wonder Nobel prize author Ernest Hemingway, after scrawling how many laboriously counted words in pencil in a Cuban attic, found himself so helpless without the fellowship of God that he couldn't face doing another word. Or that John Milton convinced himself that he could write only between October and March. Or that Virginia Woolf could walk with such horrible determination into the ocean before her home, away from the words of genius that she could not admit to, until the water filled her lungs and suffocated the last agonies of creating inside her. "Only the good writers," said Hemingway, "die young." And then he went and shot himself.

Writer, I thought. And now the whole impossible dream was coming home to roost in my illness, like a giant black hawk waiting for the carrion to empty itself of breath.

Only, you see, the breath did not quite empty out.

Which I think and believe, makes the difference between despair and working again.

Especially working for my Lord Christ again.

It does not make much sense to stop writing, or living, when HE is there to write about or to live for.

For despair itself has to die in the presence of Someone who is so everlasting, so understanding, so forgiving. *Even when we simply cannot find it in ourselves to forgive ourselves, to see ourselves as he sees us — he forgives us.* Though our own hearts condemn us, God is greater then our hearts.

That is really what depression is all about. That is what Christian self-concept has to deal with.

And Jesus Christ the Lord is what going on living — and writing — is all about.

If you're going through a Death Valley of your own right now, and if you haven't found your own Harry Rinefort, I don't blame you if you feel like despairing at being "trapped" by a daily round. Nothing I can say will make you see your situation otherwise, bring understanding appreciation from your boss or your husband or your wife, or bestow on you an instant self-image that will make your mirror light up like a Rembrandt.

But if you are in love with your church, you have a flow of living water alive in your veins. You know that Doctor Harry Rinefort is talking with you, too, when he presses your shoulder to drive home this truth of you own faith: *Eternal life is pressing in on you from all sides.* Your good and gracious Lord Christ will not leave you alone. He loves you.

Really now, what more could you possibly want?

60

Even for Christians
— It Still Hurts

Life eternal is seeping into our very marrow, where-
ever we are, from whatever corner of the place where
we are.

Life eternal is finally the healer that our Lord
Christ wraps around our lives, like hot towels around
strained muscles, to soften and warm our most painful sighs with an infinite healing.

Yet this fact itself has tended to make nervous
illness suspect among some Christians.

If faith in our Lord Jesus Christ, who holds life
eternal in his hands, can help us in recovering from a
nervous breakdown, then isn't it the opposite — a lack
of such faith — that brings on the nervous problems
in the first place?

Sure. If we are willing to pass exactly the same
verdict about appendicitis. About tuberculosis. About
ulcers. About heart disease. Or about cancer.

Everything in modern medical research is going in
the same direction as far as nervous affliction is concerned. The disease is chemical in nature, genetically

determined, and as physically *real* as a tumor. It doesn't really require much genius to realize that if an illness reacts to such a solid, earthy substance as a tranquilizer, something basically physical is being treated.

Our Federal government, with a foresight quite remarkable in the progress of national medical treatment anywhere in the world, quietly agreed to the *physical* nature of nervous illness in one simple step. The government voted to include nervous infliction in the Social Security program for the disabled.

In other words, although mental breakdown is tied to your self-concept, it's more than that. It's physical too. And pain is only heaped upon pain when suffering believers are told, "You've got to believe more!" As if the God-given gift of faith can be conjured up by an act of the will! Rather it comes through the Holy Scriptures. And the gift of recovery — like the gift of faith — is just that, a *gift* from the Giver of all good things.

Wisdom from the Ozarks

Through the years in which I wrote the Bible study books for the high school youth of my church, I managed to get up early enough Sunday mornings to drive the one hundred-twenty miles south on US 66 (now Interstate 244) to an Ozark chapel. There I led the worship for anywhere from four (first service) to two hundred-twenty of the most devout Christians I have ever loved, admired, feared and thanked for their unfailing guarantee that I would always be rewarded with enough food and fuel to get me home.

The teen-agers and the hill folk both survived. To boot, while I did the writing and preaching I kept a notebook for jotting down those marks of mental health that I observed in my Ozark friends. In Pilot Knob, Missouri, survival was no simple matter. There wasn't even a last picture show to mourn about in Pilot Knob — only an ancient weatherbeaten hill, without pilots any more, not since the turn of the century, if the century ever bothered to turn there.

But none of this phased the Ozark faithful, who nourished a contentment and zest for life that made Pilot Knob a place I used to dream of while I sat in the office glaring at manuscripts for a magazine called *Spirit*, which ought to have had more of it. But I could always pull out my sweaty notebook and refresh myself with the *Commandments According to an Ozark Preacher's Notebook*.

I learned these secrets of long and happy and stubborn living from the organist in my Ozark chapel. Melda has had something like twenty-three operations. But she is not about to die young.

One. If your life-style smothers the scope of your play-interests, forget your life-style and take a flat boat trip down (or up) the Meramec, or the nearest creek. You can't get bored on a flatboat, because it isn't flat.

Two. The excitement of healing always brings with it a breath of something-I've-never-appreciated-before. The something may be a piece of seedy real estate (like my defunct lot at Lake Tishomingo), a sports car two sizes too small for your legs and/or bottom (like my Corvette, which my wife made me sell immediately after we got married), or a woman two sizes too big for your ego.

Three. Make pot-bellied stove friends with the doctor, even if the only answers he has to your problems are the "nerve pills" he ordered last March when he found his pill book hidden under his seed catalogue in the outhouse.

Get to know him well enough to tell him he's an oasis of Ozark spring water in a land of dried-up prunes. He is.

Avoid the lure of the Big Fee and the Fat Promise. I've met everyone from Freudian specialists to chiropractic faith-healers. The best doctor I've ever seen is my home-loving D. O. who did the preface for these pages. And he (to show you how old-fashioned he is) wouldn't take a penny from me for filling out all the nonsensical medical insurance forms. These he had to labor over at night, hacking away on a beat out portable. He knows more medicine by instinct than a computer could teach him in a millenium.

Four. If you have only fifty cents left to your name, spend it on a diary (with lock and key if you can't write Greek). Then record every foray to Woolworth's as if it were an African safari.

Five. Each morning — first thing — write down the one jewel you're going to put into your priceless velvet bag of jewels by the time you go to sleep at night. Make *some* kind of entry. I don't care if you have to push some paper through your typewriter like a rubber duck through a meat grinder. Just get that jewel-for-the-day locked into your semi-conscious skull via the plain old written syllable.

You'll be surprised at how your creaky mind starts grinding into gear when you put it down that *there's something to exist for.* Pretty soon you might even be smiling at the thought of your escapade. It may be something as emboldening as a walk through the boat show in a nearby mall. Or it may be buying a rose and a card for that widow down the street who pushes a shopping cart and wears black and doesn't say hello to anyone but the cat.

Six. Rejoice in the chemical changes that pitch and toss your moods. Variety is spun gold. Pray that your M. D., D. O., or neighborhood confidant goes fishing often enough to inform you, in his own quiet way, that his boat is better for him — and you — than any stethoscope, couch or boiler-maker. More patients have recovered because their doctor went cruising than from all the wise nods of the heads at Bellevue.

Seven. Avoid the phone like the Black Death. I don't care if you've got a direct line to the Mayo Clinic, the Black Monster: A) Keeps you indoors, maybe even in bed. B) Lies to you that people can really share themselves with you over a piece of plastic. C) Passes on to you all the semi-invalid bacteria carried like a pestilence by those wretched souls who think they can, or should, maneuver others to their bidding by their telephone personality.

No, I beseech you. Go. Find your way out of that musty garage. Visit. Write lettters. Plant a White Birch tree. Buy an orangutan. But make yourself some company that isn't the phony lie of the lying phone.

Eight. After you finish absorbing all the sage advice in this book, cross out in your mind every iota of counsel you've received since first you found yourself quivering with nervous trouble. *You're* going to make *your* choices now — with God's help. Start by saying a fond farewell to your official advisors. They are as helpful to you as President John Kennedy's battery of experts were to him before the invasion of Cuba. Start a file with three large brown manila envelopes: PAST. OVER. DONE WITH.

Nine. As for other written records — what about those?

Keep one. Keep the one that Jesus Christ loved, and read, and quoted when he was going through the worst of all worsts: Golgotha.

And remember, he *lived* after that.

So will you.

His Grace Is Sufficient

Besides Harry Rinefort there was a fine young doctor named Robert Gardner, who worked hard to help
me.

But he was killed on a dirt road on the Baja rocks of
Mexico. They could not allow the casket to be opened
on his broken body.

After a few days, one could possibly stand to think
about it. A thirty-five-year-old surgeon might risk his
hands motorcycling in the Southwest deserts. How
much of a scrape, even against a building, would it
take to make a hand useless for life? But there was no
wife, no child. The young doctor could laugh before
shifting his finely trained muscles up into a Volks-
wagen station wagon, to get to the motorcycle and
the hard sand.

The questions go on. But they are dead questions.

Once you start walking in it, the wasteland is endless. More empty than the Baja. More starved of
water than Sahara.

I look with Ingrid at the closed memorial to my
young doctor. The dry and the parched and the crack-
ing wounds of past days try to open again, and cannot.

We are content to walk out of the funeral home without remembering too closely the other faces that move across the inner eye. It is no use recounting them here. You have your own album of lives. We both have.

We both know pain, and shock, and terror. No one ever walks alone through downtown Detroit on a rainy night any more, or stands in front of an emptied New York theater after the play is done. It doesn't matter. We are all alone when it comes to facing into the stark void and blackness.

I go with Ingrid to our home. Not to write about the black or the rock or the sand. We know those well enough.

There are things to be looked for in all this.

There are things to be said.

But dear Lord Jesus Christ, where is the glory now?

I look for you in the sad rhythm of things-as-they-are, and I do not find you. Instead only the dullness and the aching, just the same as before.

This I do not understand, my Savior, no matter how many years I might live through it. How can the rocks and the desert of one man's sudden passing bring on the emptiness where even my faith seems cold and hard as frozen sand?

What do I need to do to see that my hold on you grows mighty and unshaken at just that moment when disaster rocks me?

See, my Lord Christ, how I start.

The question is wrong. I start with me. What do I need to do?

When all along, my great and final Friend, the issue rests with you.

For where would I be, but that you had acted first?

So that is where I start, my own Redeemer.
Here is where I start.
With you.

You.

The moment I had put that "With you" to paper, I started to feel the entrance of light.

It is the same that is promised in the Psalms.

It is a lighting and a warming that comes at me like particles of rainbow, directly out of the sun.

I try to set down more, even while the car is warming up for the drive from the funeral parlor.

> Grace is the kindest word.
> Then Thanks.
> Then Yes.
> And all of them, with Joy,
> Are melted together in Peace.

And Peace? Well, isn't that Peace — only to *be* with Jesus Christ?

I think so. If I did not, there would be no looking at the locked wood frame around the crushed form of the young doctor.

Another image moved like a shadow across the screenlike fabric of thought. There was that other doctor. He hands me a small, red-leather Nicolo Machiavelli, *The Prince.*

"This is my Bible," the doctor says.

This doctor does not sign the register at Hibbard's Funeral Home. But then, why should he? Why should he sign any such book of concern for anyone?

Nicolo would not bother. Nicolo would be out on the streets, dealing with a smile for votes. (Even if he did, as I recall, end up spending a bit too much of his life in prison and torture and, finally, disgrace.)

"This is my Bible," the also-young German doctor said.

Maybe he needs more book shelves. I got to my feet, still holding my gift-copy of Nicolo Machiavelli, and walked out to my car. There were strange beads of sweat on my forehead.

I had not felt such sweat since another day.

Really, though, it was night. A night not long before the final shattering of the breakdown.

I can no longer even regret that it happened. After it was done, four years after, I was able to say to my father, "Once I felt, *There is no way God can possible bring good out of this. When I learned different, through Ingrid, I was on the way to healing.*"

But then, four years before that, quick divorce had been very much in vogue.

There were many temptations. For a pastor's wife, there were the added appeals of money not available to her on a minister's income. Money to give her children the things that otherwise seemed out of reach. The peace of privacy. The nicety of being out of the limelight of either a parish or a parsonage. Perhaps no woman can completely ignore these things. Perhaps I was completely naive to expect that anyone could.

Perhaps I'll never know just what lay behind the goodbye, the sudden opening of the family room door, the swift, "*Honey, I'm leaving you.*" The loading of a borrowed truck in the orange-yellow light by the sliding back doors. The taking of what furniture could be got into the van. The car grinding slowly down our winding front driveway into the street we had walked together so many nights. *Honey, I'm leaving you. Goodbye.*

In all this, too, the kindest word is Grace.

But dear Lord Christ, how is it possible to remember that orange and yellow light without pain?

Yes, the good. The good did surely come from it. I know that now — better than I have known anything, ever, in all my life.

But the pain. How do you explain the pain, Lord?

But, you say, haven't you experienced enough that I don't have *to explain?*

I stand sheepish before my own understanding. You are right, of course. As you are always right. I babble about the pain when you have repaid me a thousand times in purest gold for every second of it.

It seems like a miracle, though, to pass through something you are sure will do you in — and then emerge from it with all the warmth of your Sun on my back. It seems almost like something I could never believe could be again that way.

Yet I know in my deepest levels that precisely this was the point and the purpose of all that did happen.

That I should *know — should realize once and for all and forever — that there is* nothing, *absolutely nothing, beyond the scope of your wisdom to bring good from it.*

Bring *good?*

Make *good!*

So now I make confession, my Savior.
I have been faithless. Too blind to my own faith to see.
To look into the Sun.
But now I look.
And I do not grow blind.

72

And the Lord said unto me, "My Grace is sufficient for thee: for my strength is made perfect in weakness."

The Letter

When I called Doctor Harry Rinefort that night, somewhere near ten o'clock, he was still working on the letter.

He read it to me while the words were still warm in the typewriter, but ready for another painfully thorough going-over in the morning.

October 17

To Whom It May Concern:

Re. The Reverend Walter H. C. Riess.

It has been my pleasure, and my privilege, to have known and cared for Rev. Walter Riess through one of the most trying health problems to face the human race.

His progress has been slow but immensely satisfactory, although some rather stern measures have been evoked to achieve this goal. Pastoral and other tensions and pressures are what brought this man to his very low health state, so we have had to reduce these factors or eliminate them whenever and wherever possible.

There can be no more parish pastorates; there must be no mandatory daily deadlines to meet; visits of houseguests of any nature must be limited to not over ten days; and Rev. Riess must be allowed elbow room in both time and space to write when he is so moved, and for the length of time his strength will allow.

Thanking you for your cooperation in this problem, I remain,

Respectfully yours,

(Signed)

Doctor Harry E. Rinefort

While he read I looked down at a page on my desk. A few lines in a notebook; something for the night winds.

I asked Harry Rinefort how I could say thanks. For such a gift of life that only the most incisive of medical minds could know how necessary the letter was. For each word of it reflected the precise truth, which only an instinctively brilliant physician could possible have assembled from the envelopes filled with laboratory and office data before they were brought to him.

There was a quiet laugh, hardly more than a smile, on the other end of the line.

"Pastor Riess, you did pay me," Doctor Harry said. "Don't you remember? The examination? The treatment?"

Of course I paid him. Exactly ten dollars. And for such a fee I was welcomed into the office like more than a brother, examined, counseled, and granted two hours-plus of a therapy worth at least twice the cost of driving three hundred miles with my wife Ingrid to get there.

Doctor Harry could have billed me ninety dollars for those two hours. I knew it, and he knew it.

I felt a little stunned. But why, really? The fact is that right in front of me the lines stared up at me, out of the depths of my own boyhood. Days still breathing out of the depths of my own boyhood. Days still breathing in the North Michigan air, when a boy could believe that the good Lord and Savior Jesus Christ might still — today — make a lightning difference in the quality of every heartbeat sending blood through your vessels and into your brain and into your being. After all, didn't Jesus teach us, "Except ye be converted, and become as little children, ye shall not enter the kingdom of heaven"?

There it was. Doctor Harry on the line, and the notebook of my own words in front of me:

> See
> This simple, sure-legged
> Flat word of the saint:
> Twice thought through
> Before once said —
> If then.

So at last Ingrid met the doctor in his den.

We went the next morning. For the first time in our marriage she talked with someone I thought of not only as a friend but as a Christian giant.

I have known only a few. And each time I talked with one of them, or now and then had the pleasure of hearing a talk off the cuff by one of the small group, I have come away with the same feeling.

It is a feeling of a thanks welling up so uncontrollably in my throat that I cannot trust my saying it.

It is the way most of us act, I think, when we get flooded with a fullness of thanks.

76

77

Ashes Into Beauty

Out on the Bay the first flecks of ice are visible. They will become mountains for people to cross, on their way to their automobiles or their fishing or whatever will bear the load of the insatiable curiosity that drives men wild in search of that condition we so easily call happiness.

I remember now some lines I wrote when all that seemed possible for me was an endless chasing around the country for specialists of one kind or another, from city suite to city suite of the health merchants of our time. When I didn't yet feel the full compelling force of a bay brightening with ice at its peaks, snow contrasting with water fighting to stay its own master.

I put it down:

It is true. I have been looking
Desperately, clamorously, with too much fury.
Somewhere I learned from some wise saint
This is the way: ths search, this quest.
Even this pain of bothering to say,
I will not let this day go by
But that I track some witness to its lair.

They smile. They say: Rest is the only way.
But yet, there is the time that's left to us
If rest we want. No,
I will not let this day go by.

So many mornings came to test these words. Why not remain in bed, when there is no cure? Why not quit looking — just for this one day?

That's not for the Christian who believes that the humblest work room becomes a garden of warmth and beauty once Christ has there opened his heart and shown how much he cares. A hospital room can be that. An emergency ward. The favorite view of William Wordsworth (like the hills across our Bay) that could make his heart leap up with joy — these surroundings are blessed by the pain that eliminates everything else from our concern.

I do not pretend to understand in the least how our Lord works this alchemy on our lives, how he turns negatives into positives, despair into rejoicing, work into play, tools into scepters, pain into happiness, ashes into beauty. But I know he does it. I know that finally this, and nothing else, is the avenue to all that really matters.

How my heart grieves for those who are still trying alternate routes. One of the saddest moments of my life occurred recently when I saw the strain and tension wrecking a close family of Christians who had chosen another route and found it empty not only of any joy, but also finally empty of the rewards in money that they sought. There is a strange despair that settles into the heart ruled by a passion unworthy of the Kingdom of God. And today it is so fearfully easy for the soul to be twisted and wracked and misled by the gaudy neon display of supposed answers to life.

One walk down the main street of any major city in America is enough to make you sick at heart, if you know where your soul is at. For the lies on the billboards do not work. Yet the lies draw people like flies to honey. And the honey is deadly poison.

I do not think it is possible for us to go through our days without being nipped by the clashing rocks of temptation. Being together on this northern bay has not freed Ingrid and me from the pain of this. But living here has freed us to be happy even in spite of the temptation. It seems that those who have elected to live away from the "motor" city and other centers of our culture manage to keep their sense of values a little more in shape. I notice in myself a sense of confusion when I visit these centers. Everyone is so busy with the art of getting and spending that there is no room left for the life oriented in God. There is no room to think of what comes first. Here, with the quietness of people who have chosen and chosen well, and live out their choice to the full, there is time to pray. I realize this even now, while I am doing this line, on a typewriter that has heard a thousand silent, intense and thoroughly answered prayers.

The Mystery of Place

Who can trace the mysterious influences of a place upon a person?

We have all had the experience of walking into a room, and sensing that we have been there before —even though that may have been impossible. I have felt this often, and I can't possibly explain the familiarity one can feel with a place never seen before. Enough to say that I have had the experience, that it has shaken me to the roots, and that it certainly does prove — if nothing else — that places occupy a more intense role in our lives than we usually admit.

We walk into a cathedral, and suddenly the aura of worship fills and surrounds our being. Our best friend may be standing at our side, but may be left completely cold by everything around. Yet we will never forget what we have seen and sensed.

One evening not so long ago Ingrid and I remembered that we had seen a certain kind of blue before.

The waters of Grand Traverse Bay, even at dusk, strike with a startling suddenness when you come toward them from the south, from behind the hills that forever shield and enfold a haven of lakes and bays.

Today I paged through the medical sheaf of papers given me within sight of the incredible blue bay where we make our home. The papers do not say return to the parish. They do not say official ministry again. They do not say absence of pain.

But — and this is a sign of the power of place — they do not say *finis*, either, to life.

What once demanded cortisone now calls for something that will not devour the body. What once drowned the spirit in overwhelming power of diagnosis and treatment — and ever-present grayness of face — now brings hope. And all the way home, along the shoreline coated with sand or snow, the words of a doctor in Detroit echo aganst a windshield clear and bright with vision.

The blue water that laps along the bay shore is the same water I heard in my boyhood. I have a sense that my soul has been fixed to this one star of the north since I was born. It is a conviction knit with faith.

I do not have to add that there have been, and are still, threats of a sort — even to a conviction of faith. Yet the conviction of faith is more persistent. And if a rumor intrudes, there is always the breaking through of the same light that started our journey back — and forward: "If he slay me, yet will I trust him."

Thank the Lord I am not immune to that, either. It is, in fact, the content of my days.

Even the first hope, of course, did not happen overnight. I have seen healing come that way. A noted surgeon of St. Louis told me of startling resurrections of spirit that he had seen in more than one patient — revivings that left him shaken and weak in the face of all the knowledge he had gathered to himself in the course of becoming the doctor he was.

I have my own list of such events, almost impossible to describe completely. For many wise reasons, the church has always chosen to place itself on the doubting side of the reports of miracle healings. It is probably better that way. And yet — sometimes I wonder how many Christians have given up simply because that silence of some church dimmed their own vision of their lives' purpose. Shadowed their sense of the presence of God, their idea of an eternity really within reach! Shaded the mystery of place, *the place*.

Why did God ask Abraham to leave Ur of the Chaldees for "a land that I will show thee" — when God could have made Ur of the Chaldees itself the Center of His Presence? Why all that wandering of Israel in the dryness of the desert for all those dry, dry years, just to find another part of the desert on the Mediterranean? None of this makes any possible sense — unless there is a particular place where he *wants* to break through, and love, and heal, and make a stronger impact of himself on our lives so dead and dreary without him.

It is all a wonder beyond our knowing. The Angel of the Lord stirs the waters at the Pool of Bethesda, and nowhere else. In our youth we fall in love with a place — a place surrounded by the beams of a cottage attic — and we must return there to live, even if a doctor says there is no time left to make such a life possible.

But there is time.

That is the final word of a land where I find it easier to pray.

The way to healing may last all of life, and end only in the perfection of eternity. But the way lies through the place God gives us to be, no matter what the deserts, no matter what the discomforts and obstacles.

The way is real. The way is even good.

The way is filled with the saying of thanks..

In the Company of Healing

If you were to take a poll, chances are that no one, with the possible exception of Bob Hope would stand higher as a healer of America's spirit than Jack Benny.

The man looked for all the world like he owned any stage he set foot on. Week after week he appeared before the whole nation as the very essence of ease and relaxation — "grace under pressure," as one critic termed his art. The timing of his stories was the stuff of legends. His long, perfectly paced pauses. His greatest of all laughs came at the time he said absolutely *nothing* — while a thug was holding a gun to his back and demanding, "Your money or your life."

It wasn't until after he died that his wife Mary revealed what Jack himself never talked about while he was convulsing audiences with his maddening, almost bored-looking silences.

Jack, she said, chewed his fingernails to the nub just reading the manuscript of a program in planning. He paced the living room, refused to eat, lost his temper all out of character for the gentle soul regularly victimized by a world that sneered at his Maxwell and his bank vault.

How many victims of nerves waited every week for a Jack Benny special to calm their befuddling anxieties, never imagining that the relaxed victim of their own world of frustrations was quivering in the face of his own tensions — which more than once approached

the boiling point?

On another network, over the longest period of time ever endured by a television comedian, appeared a fellow named Red Skelton. Red didn't seem as poised and cool as Jack Benny, but he had to master an act in a class by itself just to go before the lights. Red Skelton vomited repeatedly before every performance, often tried to escape from studio commitments, and when he went home at night kept every light in the house burning through his endless repeated nights of sleeplessness.

These were the on-top manipulators of public taste in humor. Behind such visible figures stood others, such as the finest college platform speaker I have ever heard — no matter what the stage or event. "O. P." was in constant demand from his university and in a wide circle beyond. We asked him to speak at one of our seminary student forums, too.

We were all there, waiting for the educator to emerge from the sheath of red velvet drapes. But O. P. failed to make it through. Instead, the dean of the chapel hurriedly threw together a fine speech somewhere near the announced theme of the celebrated guest-to-be, and afterward I cornered the dean long enough to find out what happened to O. P.

O. P., it turned out, suffered violent attacks of the sweats and nausea and extreme shortness of breath before going out to meet even student audiences. This time — not the first time by far — he couldn't make it. He begged the dean to step into the breach, which the dean could do, and did, while O. P. hustled out the side door to call a cab.

The deeper point is, however, that O. P. went back to his teaching. He didn't use the back door to dodge his way "all the way to Timbuktu," as one of my fellow editors threatened — at least once a week — to do. And Jack Benny did not quit his specials. And Red Skelton did not give up because of the weekly bouts with nausea. They kept going, sometimes in an anguish of mind and spirit that no one else could suspect.

I don't have to retrace the opposite situations. The Jack London who killed himself with the bottle. The W. C. Fields who really did run away from the specials — even those outside of Philadelphia. The Joe McCarthy, who let millions of supporters cry themselves to death with him. The Wordworths and the Coleridges who quit writing because of some demonic idea that their poetry had to be something superhuman. Amid the rampant millions who have tried to fight their way alone through the fright and fraught of breakdown, the list of the defeated is beyond count.

But the list is not beyond the reach of a few contagious Christians who — in their quiet, unpretentious company — help to heal the spirit of anyone in grief. All this company has going for it is the inner awareness of the invisible and utterly secret power of faith. This Scripture-based faith the chosen few prize above rubies — a fact which never ceases to astound, confound, and frustrate those who deal in rubies.

Melda, for one, hidden away in Ironton in the Ozarks, would not think a second thought about "just being rich." The Ozark home of hers looks like an

Ozark night wind, of the kind that comes sweeping through the small mountain towns with their smoking log cabins, and might flatten in an instant her life savings. I've had the pleasure of being there for coffee many Sunday afternoons, and I've heard another side of Ozark living past me from a nearby farm where they made damson juice down by the creek bed. Out there too hanged the venison, waiting for winter in the smokehouse. But nobody will tell the preacher who it was who last sat out on a limb just before dawn, measuring with practiced eyes the deer on the path below as they flicked past like ghosts on the way to the concealed (and slightly illegal) salt licks.

"The sweetest and best Winchesters ever invented, those salt licks," an Ozark farmer told me on one of those autumn afternoons drenched in the peculiar light-gray shadows cast by scrubby trees going now to speckled red and yellow on the stubby hillsides where the deer-traps are hid. I never did stumble across a single one, no matter how often or how long I dared to walk along the spider's web of pathways worn into the woods. By how many winter boots? Side-trees brushed by how many threadbare jackets that somehow kept carrying the antique rifles that brought down the deer when meat prices soared so high that stores "might just as well move to the city," along with the coffee, sugar and whisky.

In the midst of this austere mountain greenery lived Melda, scratching out her day's journal on linen parchment — the only kind the grocery store handled. Melda's secret is safe. She has kept her hold on sanity by the courageous decision to pour herself out on vellum, whether she has any money left for stamps for manuscript-mailing (and in the Ozarks she may not) and whether anyone bothers to match her courage by answering or not.

Because the backbone of Melda' determination is courage. It takes a lot of that to believe that what you're doing in Ironton, Missouri is worth taking up paper with. But I can't think that Melda would give two hoots and a holler in Pilot Knob Valley to ascertain all that the sages of the New York press might judge her writing to be. A few times she did ask me to go over this or that bit of copy, such as some side-history of the Pilot Knob battlefield during the Civil War. She accepted what few comments I had to make with a dignity and a silence that made *me* feel honored to see the manuscript, although it was perfectly possible that I was the only one who ever read her story.

But I believe I *was* the honored one. I have done my share of writing-for-these-eyes-only, and I know what it is to clutch a sheaf of papers under my arm, lest some judge should lay upon it the weight of the wisdom of the world. Even in the years of the office that fear occurred to me more than once. I hung on to the writing (I won't say more; the words weren't that good) and toted my loaded attache' case where angels fear to tread, namely among the absolutely bankrupt typewriter pages stacked alongside the office typewriter which I had somehow managed to cajole from the purchasing agent of the publishing house.

But even though the typewriter — an executive machine with variant spacing for different letters at that — kept breaking down, I did persist enough to squeak through the jungle of the white pages, just as Melda made it through hers. It is still a constant excitement to me how the unending care and concern of our Lord Jesus Christ comes through the frustration to bless those hardy souls who dare to slip a sheet of paper into the typewriter for the sake of capturing their convictions on paper.

I don't care how you carry it off. But if Jack Benny and Red Skelton could keep acting, if O. P. could keep teaching, if Melda can keep writing in the Ozarks and if I can do it at home, then you can do it too. Take a portable antique into Death Valley; words can grow in withered sand. Get thee to a stationery store. Find thee thine own book store. Pay out thine uttermost farthing for a charcoal sketch pad. If anyone, even your doctor, tries to put the chloroform to it, smile and buy a new cartridge for your ink pen on the way out.

I am not asking you. I am not setting you up with an impossible dare.

I am simply saying that if you do *not* express yourself *some*where, to *some* empty sheet of paper, or possibly to *some* lost aunt who maybe won't bother to let you know her most recent address in her most recent retirement village, you're killing yourself off by inches.

That's like treating your breakdown with the venom of an Ozark copperhead.

If you want to learn more about that, write to Melda. I guarantee you'll get an answer. I guarantee you'll have a writing partner who'll keep you writing for life.

To her it's all part of the healing process: The company of the healing ones. The thankful ones.

The Thanks of the Lonely

I saw what the pain of loneliness is like at our last neighborhood meeting.

Next to me through four hours of empty words sat one of the marvelously efficient young women you see in New York editorial offices, maybe on the staff of *Glamor* magazine. She lives alone in a huge white Cape Cod house, where the lights stay on almost every night — a memorial to a divorce that happened God knows where for God knows what reason.

Across from me lounged a former executive of a Detroit motor firm who has moved, by his own statement, "fifteen times in the last six years." Now he is moving again. He doesn't know why. But he is moving.

The rest of the suburban parlor was filled with other monuments to the *apartness* written all over the homeowners. *Apartness* by the shores of a Grand Traverse Bay so startlingly beautiful that even now, as I write, I have all I can do to keep my eyes on the paper in front of me. We can cite all the divorce and death statistics we want. We can try to escape with the help of tidy little phrases like "The Age of Alienation." All right. But I'll still be able to prove by the vacant eyes and the hollow faces in that meeting room that the disease of *apartness*, of the kind of loneliness that our world has never seen before, is the real surging stream running underground beneath all the smaller gurgling geysers we call divorce, or separation, or mismatch, or tension-of-the-sexes, or failure, or bankruptcy or neighborhood feuding.

It is all there. In the faces. In the eyes.

A terrible hunger. A hunger for certainites.

Everyone is fighting a hard battle. But mainly to hide the symptoms, not cure the disease. Maybe if you take enough martinis at a get-together of *anybody* with *anybody*, you can start feeling for just an hour or an hour and a half that you are truly in love with *everybody*. Maybe. It doesn't always work, of course. Alcohol has the unhappy quality of unleashing your anger, too. Or making you act like a flirtatious fool. Or putting you to sleep in the corner and insulting to fury your hostess and host. Unless they too have had enough of their 9½ to ½ martinis not to care any more.

By then, though, it doesn't matter. By then the loneliness, as my German doctor used to tell me about the suburban festivals, is dissolved in a sea of alcohol.

"All anxieties, " he would say, "are soluble in alcohol."

But even that disciple of Nicolo Machiavelli couldn't really buy that solution.

He knew it all too well. He knew it from the lines of the lonely and the lost willing to wait for years to find a smattering of help at his Grosse Pointe office door. He knew, and he said it, that thanksgiving was becoming an extinct phenomenon in America. And he knew too from the very wealth of his patients that *outer* needs, *outer* wants, had nothing at all to do with the loss of thanksgiving.

And he knew, I am sure of it, that Nicolo Machiavelli had absolutely no answer for the long lines waiting at his own door.

But the other thing the German doctor in Grosse Pointe did not know.

He did not know, or did not choose to believe, that the inner secret of faith did — as Jesus Christ so often said it did — *"make thee whole."*

What is the secret of faith?

How do we put it into the coldness of words on paper, black on white, witness open to the cruelty of doubters and critics?

That is a thing that only courage can take on.

It is, at the last, only courage that can take the terribly personal burden of apartness, of loneliness.

Courage in faith does not say: *You must give me a servant to keep me company.* You can't say that to Someone who was not served at all, but *gave his life a ransom for many.*

Courage in faith does not say: *You can't leave me alone like this.* You can't say that to the God-man whose own mother sobbed helplessly while she could do absolutely not a thing for the One who hanged so totally apart on the cross.

Courage in faith says: *Come loneliness. Come apartness. I am afraid of you. But I take you to myself — like a father clasps his son — if that is the will of my Lord God.*

Courage in faith discovers in amazement that the pressing Life and Light of Jesus Christ bore all the harder on him who sees that there is no higher calling than to share the mystery of the Son of Man: *Take up your cross and follow me. . . . I have called you my friends.*

There is nothing that can follow that but thanksgiving.

What else is left? To sense in yourself that his being with you really is eternal. That he does not let you alone, ever. That to suffer apartness — *He was despised and rejected of men* — is to hug to yourself that truth that is almost beyond the reach of the ages.

> *. . . there is really no death,*
> *And if ever there was it led forward to life,*
>   *and does not wait at the end to arrest it,*
> *And ceased the moment life appeared.*
>
> *All goes onward and outward . . . and nothing collapses,*
> *And to die is different from what any one supposed,*
>   *and luckier.*

Walt Whitman was so close there. All he had to add was:

> *And his Life was the Light of men.*

But this is a hope which only the Bible can give.

You Can Go Back Again

Now and then I take the road that runs near the old cottage with the hearth and the loft.

Some distance from the cottage on Spider Lake I start to feel tempted. Find the exact place. Drive down the long straight lane leading to the lake and the rear entrance. Hope that someone is there, and that you might be shown through. Then walk up the wooden stairs into the loft, and hope it might all be still as it was then. And hope that you might be alone, for just the shadow of a moment, to take in to yourself everything as you felt it then.

The memory of that North Michigan cottage loft is engraven in me.

Suddenly in the trees there is a shimmering of sun on water, glinting through the woods just far enough to reach the dust of the road puffing up behind the car. I slow down even more, wondering if a glimpse of rustic brown might possible betray the location of the place that more than any other changed my life.

It is getting late in the day, and the same sun that danced in red patterns of promise on the windshield now threatens to leave us wandering around a lake on unmarked roads. The fishermen are already off the water. Lights start to flicker in a dozen windows hidden away in the trees. No children run along the shoreline.

"If we come to the end of the road," my wife asks, "how are we going to turn around?"

"Is it really that dark already?"

She smiles, knowing that I want only a sure view of a cabin that may have stayed as it once was, as I once knew it.

"I'm afraid it's darker than that."

I find the first driveway, almost invisible in the dusk, and turn the car sharply, almost blindly, so that we still have time to swing altogether around. The lights in the cottage below us, between us and the lake, do not seem welcoming to strangers. Years can change cabin lofts into storage rooms, or redecorated guest chambers, or places where old friendships are forgotten.

"Yes, you're right. I know." My voice is still hopeful in the darkening car. There is no flutter of images on the windshield.

But there is the fact of my own prayer loft waiting for me at home.

And what a sustaining country's heart is there.

There have been other times when I have returned to places of spiritual nourishing.

Deep in the bowels of Detroit, so deep hardly any sunshine can reach in, stands an old wooden church with two parsonages. The three buildings now carry boards in this window or that, and some doors hold planks nailed across the outside. Once they were doors we slammed with immense glee, our bags piled high on a heavy, square-built Oldsmobile squatting as if it simply could not make it north to the lakes — ever, in a day, in a year, ever.

Later on I would make return travels to Forest Park in St. Louis, and to the art museum there to which I walked in rain or snow or under the burning Missouri sun. Or to the hill there, overlooking the city, where in prayer and with a Testament in my hand I made my own ordination vows.

The mere sight of these places could, and did, send waves of familiar emotions surging through me. They were the emotions I felt the first time I recited a Psalm there, or said a prayer, or recalled a hymn. Seldom did these return visits fail to clear the waters of memory, or rekindle the warmth of devotion I felt at the beginning.

I knew instinctively, of course, that mere memory of such moments was not enough to stand up against the winds of the times that often sent me searching into the places of the past. The Christ of the cottage loft was real, but he would have to be found and worshiped in life as I build life now, today. Spider Lake, or Bethany, or Forest Park — these were places of prayer and love and discovery for me. But it was what happened there that changed my life, that led me into preaching and writing his Name in every way that I could. And it was he who finally brought me into the place where no prayer ever seemed one second wasted.

My cottage loft now is quiet, set apart, with a window that looks out across the west arm of our Bay.

I cannot step into the room without praying, any more than I can put my fingers to my typewriter without feeling in myself an unspoken psalm.

How precious are the hours spent there! Ingrid and I have made it back to the place where Jesus Christ seems most real, most present, to us. We have made it back through the wrecks of time to a place that is our own, one that is made for prayer and for life.

Who or what can threaten such a place? What can anything threaten when you have made the last commitment? When you have been guided to say inside yourself: "If he slay me, yet will I trust him"?

I know the stakes when you build among ruins. The wrecks of time do not like buildings standing among them. The buildings are an accusation, a living monument to life denied. The stakes become very quickly life and death.

But our place is built upon a thousand moments with him who is the Foundation of all that endures.

We have looked his Truth clear in the face.

We have learned his love.

What in the world is there to fear?

The Last Word Is the Word

Across the West Bay the lights mark the shore. Above them the hills loom dark and eternal. From the living room comes the muffled sound of a reporter commenting on the latest cataclysmic change in world power balance.

I look again at the hills and the Bay. All color is gone from them now. Yet they remain massive and untouched by the last telecast out of Washington. "I will look unto the hills, from whence cometh my help," wrote David, "My help cometh from the Lord, which made heaven and earth." And King David rests from his labors, all the cataclysm about him shaken into dust.

But his word — the Word — remains. No, it is more than ever the touchstone of those who see, as one television commentator put it, that "nothing is predictable any more."

Those of us who have grown up with the Bible, who have borne that Word inside ourselves from the cradle, do not and cannot realize the treasure we have in this earthen vessel. We struggle to reach out to each other with a word from God's Word. We stammer and stutter and tremble in our trying. And all the time we do not see that it is not we who have to do all the trying, all the trembling, all the anticipating of what will work, this method or that, this format or that.

In the middle of the illness in which, and perhaps through which, I came to this north country, I made a vow with my Lord that I have tried to carry through.

Each day in my study on West Bay, I would set down on paper — no matter how great my inner frailty, the best word I have to say of him. I will keep that word circulating as well as I can. But I will not strain to "sell" that word, or to back it with "personality," or to make sure that it gets "adequate attention."

I have turned that job over to my Lord and Savior Jesus Christ, permanently and without reservation. He is a living, gracious and all-controlling Friend — and nothing I have gone through can change that.

The grave far below Space Craft One — the grave where they once laid the body of my crucified Savior — is indeed empty.

You see, he is here with me.

With us.